The Debt-Free *Diet*

A 12-WEEK GUIDE
TO FINANCIAL FITNESS

KC Moog

The Debt-Free Diet

Copyright © 2017 by KC Moog All rights reserved

No part of this publication may be reproduced, stored in a retrieval system, or transmitted in any way by any means, electronic, mechanical, photocopy, recording or otherwise without the prior permission of the author except as provided by USA copyright law.

This book is designed to provide accurate and authoritative information with regard to the subject matter covered. This information is given with the understanding that neither the author nor FCE Publishing is engaged in rendering legal, professional advice. Since the details of your situation are fact dependent, you should additionally seek the services of a competent professional.

Published by   FCE Publishing   Atlanta, GA
Published in the United States of America
ISBN-13: 978-197775-8729   ISBN-10: 19775872X
   Business & Economics: Personal Finance: Budgeting/General

"People who have financial difficulty, devise hundreds of *excuses* for their problems and are *afraid* to really look at their situation openly, *hoping desperately* that it will somehow go away.

In my twenty-five years, I have worked with thousands of folks who were overwhelmed with their money woes. I regret they did not have this book to guide them out of their self-made pit.

I have also witnessed the great results of people's honest assessment of their situation and then taking control of the money they do have. This book can change lives!"

Billie Ward

Facilitator of Better Living on a Shoestring,
Eviction Prevention Program
Stonington, Connecticut,
Dept. of Human Services

TABLE OF CONTENTS

07 ✦ Introduction

13 ✦ Week One: Step on the Scale

23 ✦ Week Two: Calories In vs. Calories Out

35 ✦ Week Three: The Frozen Dinner

41 ✦ Week Four: It's Time to Lose Some Weight

47 ✦ Week Five: The Weekly Weigh-In

55 ✦ Week Six: Some Favorite Recipes

67 ✦ Week Seven: The Occasional Treat

73 ✦ Week Eight: Beware of Temptations

79 ✦ Week Nine: Keep All Food on the Table

85 ✦ Week Ten: Conquering Setbacks

95 ✦ Week Eleven: Exercise

107 ✦ Week Twelve: Congratulations! You Did it!

117 ✦ Appendix I

121 ✦ Appendix II

INTRODUCTION

WHY DEBT FREE?

Think about it for a moment. I mean, *really* think about if you didn't owe any debt (not even a mortgage). What would your weekly or monthly take-home income be? That's a lot of extra money, isn't it? Imagine what you could do with that money. That is money with which you could do the things you have always dreamed about: start a college fund for one of your children or grandchildren; own a home; see a part of the world you have always dreamed about visiting; make some investments; open a small business. Whatever dreams that debt keeps you from achieving, these things could be yours!

Think about how much stress debt causes in your daily lives. How much physically healthier would you be if you were financially healthy and debt free?

Think about how much stress could be eliminated from your relationships if you were debt free. How much happier would you and possibly your family be if you weren't burdened mentally with debt? In fact, many sources cite household debt as one of the leading causes of failed marriages.

Being debt free may also give you the freedom to change careers and help you not to feel trapped in your current position because of the bills you owe.

True financial health can come only when you have lost the weighted burden of debt.

WHY TWELVE WEEKS?

Many nutrition experts agree that most people can stick with a dieting goal for twelve weeks. This is what I am asking you to do. Commit to yourself that for the next twelve weeks you are going to stick with this no matter what and see just how exciting financial fitness can be!

OVERVIEW

Each week you will be asked to read each chapter and, as best as you can, do what it says to do. You will have to trust that I know what I am talking about. Otherwise, it is like asking a doctor for a prescription but not taking it. The medicine will not do you any good if it sits in the bottle. Likewise, this plan will not do your finances any good if you don't put it into action. This concentrated effort over the next twelve weeks will create several healthy financial habits that will lead you to establishing a new lifestyle. Once you are comfortable in this new lifestyle and begin to reap the many rewards, you will stay on the right track toward true financial health and the achievement of your personal goals!

Here is a list of some helpful information before we get started:

✦ You may find it helpful to read through all of the lessons completely before starting to work through them individually so that you have an understanding of how it will ultimately all come together.

✦ Each week you will need one or two hours to work through the lesson.

✦ I suggest that you pick a set time and make a commitment to that time. (For example, Sunday afternoons from 2 p.m. to 4 p.m.) Plan your other weekly obligations around it just as if you are taking a class or as if you have an appointment.

I know that many of you are wondering, "What does debt have to do with dieting?" Well, quite a bit, actually. Over the years, many of you have probably learned the basic dieting techniques and may even understand why they work effectively. As you will soon learn, controlling your money takes a lot of the same skills as controlling what you eat (self-discipline, controlling emotional impulses, and planning ahead, just to name a few).

Don't worry! If you have failed or only succeeded temporarily on diets before, I will show you how to avoid the common pitfalls and traps. The good news (for all of us) is that you can learn to successfully control your money much faster and easier than you can learn to control your eating habits! I will show you how to succeed and how simple it is to apply these same techniques of proven success to controlling your finances.

IN TWELVE SHORT WEEKS, YOU WILL:

- ✦ successfully be living within you means
- ✦ have saved $500 for an emergency
- ✦ have a written plan for reducing and eliminating *all* debts
- ✦ know several creative ideas on speeding up your debt elimination process
- ✦ have learned to avoid common pitfalls and traps

By committing to this program, you are taking that so-important first step toward feeling the freedom of being debt-free and in control of your own finances! I am so excited that you have chosen to take this journey—a journey toward debt elimination and true financial health!

Are you ready to get started toward the new financial you? Then, let's go!

WEEK ONE:

STEP ON THE SCALE

What are three things you must know before starting a financial diet?

1. What your current financial situation is
2. What being financially healthy means to you
3. What you hope to accomplish

Just as with a weight-loss diet, first you must step on the scale and determine what real financial weight you are carrying. This assessment is critical in order to determine what your financial goals are.

In order to determine your financial weight, you will need to list all of your assets (positive numbers) and all of your liabilities and obligations (negative numbers).

For our purposes, an asset is anything that has value that is in your name (a car, a house, a whole-life insurance policy, household goods, stocks, and bonds are examples of assets). Also, for our purposes, a liability is anything that you are obligated to pay money to each month (this includes medical/dental bills, credit card payments, automobile payments, home mortgage, etc.)

See the following example

JOHN & JANE DOE'S FINANCIAL SCALE

Assets

Current value of home	$210,000
2008 Ford (current book value)	$12,000
2010 Mazda (current book value)	$4,700
401(k) (current value)	$22,000
Furniture and household goods	$8,000
Savings account	$300
Total assets	$257,000

Liabilities

Home Mortgage	$171,000
2008 Ford loan balance	$9,700
Student Loan balance	$19,000
Visa credit card balance	$6,400
Discover credit card balance	$3,200
Home Depot credit card balance	$1,400
Medical bill balance	$490
Total liabilities	$211,190

STEP ONE

Please list all of your assets and liabilities. The following is just a possible guide.

Assets

Current value of home	_____
Automobile #1 (current book value)	_____
Automobile #2 (current book value)	_____
401(k) (current value)	_____
Furniture and household goods	_____
Savings account	_____
Total assets	_____

Liabilities

Home Mortgage	_____
Home equity loan	_____
Home equity line of credit	_____
Automobile #1 loan balance	_____
Automobile #2 loan balance	_____
Furniture loan balance	_____
Medical bill #1 balance	_____
Medical bill #2 balance	_____
Dental bill balance	_____

Student loan #1 balance   _____

Student loan #2 balance   _____

Misc. loan balance   _____

Credit card #1 balance   _____

Credit card #2 balance   _____

Credit card #3 balance   _____

Credit card #4 balance   _____

Total liabilities   _____

Now that you have an accurate idea of where you are, don't get discouraged! You are now in a much better position to set informed, realistic goals for yourself.

STEP TWO

Critical issues in determining what a healthy weight is for you are things that are heavily out of balance. For example, a person with a $25,000 annual income is in a very unhealthy financial situation if they owe $40,000 on the vehicle they drive. A couple with a combined household income of $60,000 is financially unbalanced with a $600,000 mortgage. Ideally, I hope you will make the decision that any weight of debt is unhealthy to your financial situation; but that is a personal decision that you must make for yourself. (Please note: If you are married, this definition needs to be a joint decision! What weight you are comfortable carrying is not necessarily what weight your spouse is comfortable with.)

STEP THREE

Here I want you to do a little creative thinking. I am talking about setting both some short-term and long-term financial goals.

Before we do this exercise, it is necessary to make a clarification in the difference between a dream and a goal. It is very important to understand the fundamental difference in the way you think about each. Simply stated, *a goal is a dream with a deadline.*

An example of a dream is to say, "I'd like to own my own business someday." The way to turn that dream into a goal is to say, "By the end of next year (18 months from now), I am going to have saved $15,000 by saving $1,000 a month and finding a financial partner so that on *month/day/year* I can open my own ice cream parlor."

Please make sure, as you go through the following exercise, you are making *goal statements,* not just dreaming. Ideally, your first long-term goal is to be debt free for all of the reasons we discussed earlier.

I realize that, right now, being debt free may seem too far away to seem realistic. So, let's concentrate on setting some short-term, interim goals for now.

Goal#1: Don't gain any more weight! This sounds simple enough, but it is truly critical. This means that you will start living within your means and not spend any more money than you make. Not one penny more! (You will see how to do this in the next chapter.)

Goal#2: Have $500 in savings by the end of this twelve weeks. *Yes, you can!* I will show you how to do this in week three.

Goal#3: Begin systematically eliminating your debts. This is week four's lesson.

ANY PERSONAL SHORT-TERM GOALS

You may have your own goals that you would like to see happen in your financial situation in the next three months, six months, or year. Write those here **with deadlines!**

_____

_____

_____

_____

_____

_____

_____

_____

_____

_____

_____

_____

_____

_____

ANY PERSONAL LONG-TERM GOALS

Do you have goals that you would like to see happen in your financial situation in the next three to five years? If so, write those here:

_____

_____

_____

_____

_____

_____

_____

_____

_____

_____

_____

_____

Now that you have these goals in writing, you may be asking yourself, *"How do I get from where I am now to where I want to be?"* Truthfully, that is where many people fail. The reason is because they don't know that it is much more effective to ask the question in reverse: *"How do I get from where I want to be, to where I am now?"* Let's go back to our example of the ice cream parlor:

Jane has always wanted to own an old-fashioned ice cream parlor. She sets the goal that on month/day/year *she is going to open her own ice cream parlor. Then she starts brainstorming what has to happen a month before that date; six months before that date, a year before, two years before, until she gets back to today's date. She is moving from small, specific details to broad details. This ensures that details don't get overlooked.*

Now that she has a realistic plan, she can start to work her plan and achieve her goal!

IT'S YOUR TURN!

Try applying this reverse goal-planning principle to one of your short-term goals listed above.

_____
_____
_____
_____
_____
_____

CHAPTER REVIEW

By the end of this lesson you should:

- ✓ have a written list of your assets and liabilities/obligations
- ✓ know what your personal definition of being financially healthy is
- ✓ have both short-term and long-term goals written down with deadlines
- ✓ have at least one short-term goal planned out by applying the reverse goal-planning principle

WEEK TWO:

CALORIES IN vs. CALORIES OUT

Have you ever heard the saying, "If you fail to plan, you plan to fail."? Nowhere is that truer than with people's money. Money is constantly moving, and if you don't' plan where every dollar is going, then it will just be gone; and you won't really even know where it went. I'm sure you have said at least once, "I had a bunch of money, and I have no idea where it all went!" I know because I have said it myself hundreds of times!

Now, go back to what you know about dieting. Remember that we were going to take what you already know about dieting and apply it to your finances. In order to maintain a healthy physical weight, your weekly calories burned have to equal your weekly calories consumed. The same is true for a healthy financial weight. That's why this week you are going to prepare a monthly spending plan so that you account for every dollar that is coming in or going out. Some people may say, "Well isn't that a budget?"

OH NO! NOT THE B WORD!

Yes, to some degree this will be the sheet on which you "budget" your monthly financial calories (dollars), but with some very important differences than what most people think of as a household budget.

1. We will concentrate much more heavily on how many dollars you have to spend each and every month.
2. We will categorize the types of financial calories you are spending and prioritize in what order they are spent.
3. We will look at each month separately.

STEP ONE

Write down the answers to the following questions:

1. What is the *minimum* amount of salary that you earn in a month? (You may need to go back to your checkbook ledger or paycheck stubs and look at the last several months to determine an *accurate* number.)_____

2. How often do you receive that income? Monthly? Weekly? Bi-weekly?
   _____

3. Do you sometimes earn additional income? If so, how much?
   _____

STEP TWO

Make a list of all monthly expenses and categorize them into two columns:

Recurring Bills   **Disposable Debts**

Recurring bills are anything that for as long as you are living, eating, and breathing, you will have. (Examples of these are groceries, utility bills, possibly a monthly Home Owners Association fee—anything that cannot be ultimately eliminated.)

Disposable debts are any bills that could ultimately be eliminated. (Hint: The disposable debts list should be similar to what you listed as your liabilities in week one.)

STEP THREE

Now that you know how much you are earning, let's spend it! Yep, I want you to spend (at least on paper) every dollar you are going to make *for next month only*. This is known as a zero-based budget. *Before you get your first paycheck of the month,* you need to know how you are going to spend every dollar until you are back to zero again. See the following example:

John & Jane's November Spending Plan

Monthly Income	7-Nov	4-Nov	21-Nov	28-Nov
John's Weekly Salary	$1146	$1146	$1146	$1146
Jane's Weekly Salary	$1212		$1212	
Total Income	$2358	$1146	$2358	$1146
Charitable gifts	$230	$115	$230	$115
Savings				
Frozen Assets	$75	$75	$75	$75
College Fund			$50	
Housing				
Mortgage		$109	$803	$109
Utilities				
Electric	$200			
Water				$67
Gas	$124			
Phone/Cell Phone	$100			
Internet	$50			
Trash Service		$50		
Cable/Dish TV		$75		
Food				
Grocery	$179	$175	$227	$175
Dine Out	$50	$50	$15	$50

Transportation

Auto Loan			$325	
Gasoline	$75	$75	$75	$75
Repairs & Tires				
Car Insurance		$195		
License & Taxes				

Clothing

Children	$60			
Adults		$30		
Dry Cleaning				$20

Medical / Health

Disability Insurance				
Health Insurance				
Doctor Bill	$125			
Dentist				
Orthodontist	$100			
Pharmaceuticals			$15	

Personal

Life Insurance	$80	$30		
School Expenses			$75	
Art Lessons	$15		$15	
Music Lessons	$40	$40	$40	$40
Cleaning Service				

KC Moog

John's Pocket $	$40	$20	$40	$20
Jane's Pocket $	$40	$20	$40	$20
Entertainment	$30		$30	

Disposable Debts

Student Loan	$200
Home Depot®	$115
Visa®	$280
Discover®	$120

Income-Payments =	**$0**	**$0**	**$0**	**$0**

<u>Any Extra Income</u>

John's Bonus	???
Car Oil Change	$60
Jane Haircut & Color	$125
Dog Groomer	$50

Any remaining towards debt ???

Notice in the example that the bills are listed in order of John and Jane's personal importance. The first item on the plan after their incomes are entered is their contribution to their church and local charities. The next four items on their spending plan are *The Four Basic Financial Food Groups:* housing expenses, food, transportation, and clothing. Depending on your circumstances, you may need to include medical expenses (not medical bills) in your food group as well. These are the basic necessities that keep you physically, mentally, and financially healthy. *These are the things that should be taken care of first.*

Here are some other things I would like to point out from this example:

- Jane only gets paid every other week, so that is how her income is entered into their spending plan.
- John and Jane cannot pay their entire mortgage payment in one week, so they simply let the money sit in their account during weeks two and three and then pay it all at once during the last week of the month. Other bills are treated this way also.
- Jane knows they will need extra grocery money the week of Thanksgiving, so they *plan ahead* for that.
- Notice that there are some expenses on this spending plan that *could* be eliminated if things were tight. Cable television and art lessons are not basic necessities. You must prioritize for yourself what items are more important than

others.

- ✦ Finally, notice that this plan is based on a four-week month. There are going to be months where you receive more than four weeks of paychecks. These are excellent opportunities to make large payments toward your debt or frozen assets without feeling a difference in your budget.

Here are some answers to questions you may likely have at this point.

1. Why is each month treated differently?

Because they *are* different. For example, I don't have to be a psychic to know that you will probably spend a lot more money shopping in December than in other months of the year. And if you have children, you probably spend quite a bit in late August or early September on back-to-school shopping. Other months of the year have special circumstances about them as well. Do you like to go on vacation in June or July? Do you have a big birthday party for your son or daughter in February? Are your car taxes due March first? Whatever the events in your life are, they are different each month and need to be taken into consideration for each month's budget.

It is also important to know that your monthly spending plan is always going to be a work in progress. The first month's plan that you write will not be entirely accurate, and that's okay. Each month you will learn from what you did inaccurately the month before and be able to make more accurate predictions for the coming months.

Hint: One of the first things my husband, Michael, and I did to help the accuracy of our monthly spending plan was to contact the utility companies and set up a balanced pay account so that our gas and electric bills are the same amount each month. In addition, we have always maintained our contributions to our church, as a tenth of our salary, no matter how tight things were financially. I believe this to be the best biblically-sound advice anyone could take to heart. No other act will reap more financial rewards than this one (see Malachi 3:10).

2. What if I have more bills than I have money?
Well, chances are this is the case, or you wouldn't be in so much debt. Simply do the best you can. This is where you will need to set some serious priorities in your spending. Is it important to *you* (not the credit card companies) for you to eat, or for you to pay your credit card payment this month? It sounds like an obvious answer, but you might be

surprised at how many people have paid their credit card bills, but not eaten for a few days. This is why we categorized our obligations into those two categories of recurring bills and disposable debts. You need to take care of the recurring obligations before you pay the disposable debts. I will address some creative ways to fix this problem in week five.

3. What if I don't have a set income each month?
Again, here we are going to prioritize extra-income spending. You will notice in our example that there is a column of unpaid expenses at the bottom of the last page. This where that extra income needs to go. In this case, obligations, such as outstanding credit card payments should take some priority over niceties such as the dog going to the groomer.

4. If I don't pay all of my bills on time every month, won't that lower my credit score?
Possibly. But having a lot of consumer debt will lower your credit score also. And, hopefully, by the end of these twelve weeks you won't need a credit score because you won't have a need for credit.

5. If I don't pay all of my bills on time every month, won't the credit card companies call me constantly?

When Michael and I were getting out of debt, we found that if you send the credit card companies even as little as a few dollars each month, as long as their computer systems acknowledge that you have made a payment that month, it will, for the most part, keep them from calling you constantly.

IT'S YOUR TURN!

1. Please make sure you have categorized your monthly obligations into recurring bills and disposable debts.
2. Now, prioritize these bills in order of what is most important to you.
3. Write your first month's spending plan, starting with your first paycheck next month.

Note: The easiest way to set up your spending plan is in a Microsoft Excel® Spreadsheet. If you don't own Microsoft Office® on your computer, Google® provides a free version on their site also. You do not need to purchase Excel® if you do not already own it.

CHAPTER REVIEW

By the end of this lesson you should have:
✓ categorized your monthly obligations into recurring bills and disposable debts
✓ prioritized your monthly obligations in order of importance to you
✓ written a spending plan beginning with next month.

WEEK THREE:

THE FROZEN DINNER

Remember the quote last week, "If you fail to plan, you plan to fail"? Credit card companies are banking (and winning) on the fact that most people fail to plan. I'm sure you've heard someone say, "Well, I just have a credit card fro emergencies."

When Michael and I started looking at how we had accumulated our debt, we first noticed how we had **not** accumulated our debt. We had not taken an exotic vacation or bought ourselves expensive toys; we simply had not planned well. One car needed new tires; the dishwasher had be replaced; a child needed an emergency doctor visit—life events happened that were not planned for.

Much of the time, I try to keep some sort of frozen dinner in the freezer for the nights when things get crazy and I don't get home in time to cook, because nothing will blow a diet or a budget faster than an unplanned dinner out. The same holds true for your financial health. In order for you to create a healthy financial balance, those crazy times when something goes wrong must be planned for with what I call, "frozen assets."

Just a few weeks after my family and I had made a commitment to changing our spending lifestyle, our dishwasher stopped working. At the time, we didn't have any money built into our budget for something like this, and we had already gotten rid of all of our credit cards, so we lived without a dishwasher for several weeks until we were able to build the price of an inexpensive replacement into our next month's budget. If that same event occurred today, we could easily—within a few short hours—have purchased a replacement *with cash*. What's the difference between then and now? Now, we have several thousand dollars in frozen assets set aside for those inevitable events in life that just happen unexpectedly. I need to repeat that: these events are *unexpected* in their timing, but planned for as *inevitable*.

We didn't just decide one day to set aside several thousand dollars. It took us just over a year to build up to it.

This is what I am asking you to do. Beginning this week, I am asking you to somehow find a way to set aside $50 a week for the next ten weeks so that by the end of this course, you have $500 of your own frozen assets set aside for when something goes wrong. You will no longer need to rely on the credit card companies to provide that frozen dinner when you need one for those unexpected events in life.

Again, I am asking you to rearrange your priorities and make this one extremely important to your financial health. This one act will be the key secret to your financial success!

You might be asking two important questions:

1. **When is it okay to spend your frozen assets?**
A sale at the local department store does not fall under the category of "something going wrong." Now, blowing a tire on your car, which is your only transportation to your job, a child needing to go to the doctor, a pipe bursting under your sink, these are all life events that must be taken care of. Here I am qualifying the difference between "needs" and "wants." If it is truly something that you "need" then yes, that is what the frozen assets are there for and it is okay to spend them.

2. **What happens when I spend the frozen assets?**

You have to replenish them. In week four's lesson, we are going to talk about losing the weight of your debt. Once you have had a need to spend your frozen assets, you will need to temporarily stop paying down extra money on your debt and pay that money back toward your frozen assets, until the amount is back up to what you are comfortable with having set aside. (I am so sure that you will come to enjoy the security that these frozen assets bring you that you will want to eventually increase this amount to $2,000 or more; but for now, let's just get $500 set aside.)

Once you have successfully built your frozen assets back up, you can then resume following through with your debt diet.

Real life example: Michael and I had to spend our frozen assets no less than five times during our debt diet. Whether we liked it or not, life still happened. But it didn't stop us from achieving our goals! We were still able to reduce $70,000 in disposable debt and pay *cash* for two large-unit home air conditioners and a car transmission and still replenish our frozen assets. *I we could do it, you can too!*

IT'S YOUR TURN!

1. Revise your monthly spending plan so that you are able to set aside $50 a week toward your frozen assets.
2. Plan how and create a system for tracking your frozen assets.

Hint: Even though we write our frozen assets out of our checkbook as if the money has been spent, we still leave it in the account as a buffer. This saves us from worrying about the exact timing that automatic deposits or withdrawals are made in our account. When it comes time to balance the account, we simply add the amount of our frozen assets (written in on the back page of the checkbook ledger) to the amount we show as the current balance; and it will equal what the bank statement shows as our balance.

CHAPTER REVIEW

By the end of this lesson you should:
1. Understand the absolute necessity of having frozen assets set aside for when the inevitable events of life occur
2. Have revised your monthly spending plan and found $50 a week to set aside toward these frozen assets
3. Have decided how and where you are going to keep track of these assets and set aside your first week's $50 allotment toward your frozen assets.

WEEK FOUR:

IT'S TIME TO LOSE SOME WEIGHT

Finally! What you've been waiting for! This week we are going to talk about the reason we have done all of this hard work over the past three weeks: *eliminating the burden of debt and losing financial weight!*

In week two's lesson, you separated your obligations into two categories: recurring bills and disposable debts. This week we are going to concentrate on the disposable debts.

In the example, John and Jane Doe listed their disposable debts as:

Home mortgage	$171,000
2008 Ford® loan balance	$9,700
Student Loan balance	$19,000
Visa® credit card balance	$6,400
Discover® credit card balance	$3,200
Home Depot® credit card balance	$1,400
Medical bill balance	$490
Total disposable debts	**$211,190**

Using this example, John and Jane are making the minimum payments on each of these accounts. See the table below:

Loan	Balance	Monthly Payment
Home mortgage	$171,000	$1021
2008 Ford® auto loan	$9,700	$389
Student Loan	$19,000	$219
Visa® credit card	$6,400	$280
Discover® credit card	$3,200	$120
Home Depot® credit card	$1,400	$115
Medical bill	$490	$125

STEP ONE

John and Jane have committed to their debt diet, so they are going to find a way to jumpstart the process of financial weight loss. They hold a yard sale and don't eat out this month so they can completely pay off the remaining balance of their medical bill.

STEP TWO

Beginning the following month, John and Jane apply the $125 they were paying toward their medical bill each month to *the next smallest remaining balance,* which in their case would be the Home Depot® account.

STEP THREE

In the next six months, John and Jane should completely pay off the Home Depot® account. This now allows them to increase their Discover® payment by $240 which will triple the amount of this payment.

STEP FOUR

With the extra payment from their income tax return check, they are able to completely pay off the Discover® account in eighteen months. That means in just over twenty-four months, they have eliminated three of their seven disposable debts, *without altering their lifestyle!*

STEP FIVE

John and Jane are now able to add $360 ($125 from the medical bill payment, $115 from the Home Depot® payment, and $120 from the Discover® payment) a month to their Visa® payment. This will now bring the amount they are paying toward their Visa® payment to $640 a month. As you can see, this will very quickly reduce this debt as well, especially when you take into consideration that they have already been making payments toward this bill for the past twenty-four months!

This is the power of pooling your resources! By adding one trickle at a time, you will quickly have a powerful cash flow that will change your debt situation!

Here you are probably asking an obvious question: "Twenty-four months! Can't we do it faster than that?" And the answer to that is, Absolutely! I am just showing you an example of how it can be done without making any drastic changes in your current lifestyle, but just by simply being careful with the money that you are already spending. In lesson six we are going to look at several ways to dramatically accelerate this process.

IT'S YOUR TURN!

Please list your disposable debts with the monthly payments from largest to smallest below:

_____

_____

_____

_____

_____

_____

_____

_____

_____

_____

_____

_____

_____

CHAPTER REVIEW

By the end of this lesson you should have:

✓ A list of your disposable debts with the remaining balances and monthly payments listed as well. *Hint:* It will be easier to see the order in which the debts are to be eliminated if the list is arranged in descending order according to the remaining balance.

✓ An initial plan as to how you are going to systematically eliminate these debts.

✓ Set aside your second week's allotment toward your $500 of frozen assets for a total of $100.

WEEK FIVE:

THE WEEKLY WEIGH-IN

For many people trying to lose physical pounds, it is necessary to do a weekly weigh-in. This allows them to see if they have made any progress and to be able to track their progress by recording it on a chart.

In the beginning, we asked you to set a weekly appointment to work through each lesson. Just as with a food diet or with an exercise plan, you will be more successful at keeping these appointments if you are meeting with someone else and they are holding you accountable for your attendance. I am going to call this person your accountability partner.

In order for you to stay on target with your financial goals, I suggest that you apply both of these practices to your debt reduction diet.

THE WEEKLY MEETING

At your regularly scheduled weekly meeting, you should begin by recapping what progress you made during the past week. *I cannot emphasize enough how much the positive affirmation of your real progress will motivate you to keep going!*

This is also a good time to touch on any mishaps or unexpected events that happened during that week. This will help you to formulate a plan on how to handle that situation now and plan for its recurrence in the future if necessary. As I said before, your monthly spending plan is always going to be a work in progress. It will need constant supervision and revision in order to function at its highest efficiency.

THE ACCOUNTABILITY PARTNER

For most people, your accountability partner will be your spouse. There are some occasions, however, when a couple will still require someone else to hold them accountable.

Real-life example: I worked with one couple who used the wife's father as their accountability partner. The couple found that they were unable to be disciplined even with each other, and they were wise enough to recognize this and ask for outside help.

There are four criteria your accountability partner must meet:

1. Your partner must care about your successful debt reduction as much as you do.
2. Your partner needs to feel the same way about debt and money as you do, or at least be willing to keep you on the path of the goals, you have set for yourself.
3. Your partner needs to feel comfortable enough with you to be honest with you when he or she feels you are not making a smart decision or could be doing something better.
4. You must be comfortable enough with your partner to be 100% honest when talking to him or her about money.

This can be very difficult when it comes to *how* we handle money. Money evokes very powerful emotions, many of which are deeply personal.

This can also be very difficult when it comes to *talking* about money. Many of us were taught as children that money is a very private subject and should not be discussed openly. We have to acknowledge these deeply rooted belief systems and then find a way to overcome them in order to learn the steps necessary to tackle our own issues with debt.

Real-life example: Sometimes the way we spend money is actually being generated by a deeper emotion or belief system. I worked with one man who always had to purchase the top-of-the-line, most expensive brand of a product, no matter what the item.

This man's decision-making process was actually being generated by a deep-seated frustration stemming from his childhood when his father would only buy the cheapest models of everything. Consequently, the man always had to deal with toys, appliances, and cars that never worked the way they were supposed to or at least not for very long.

It took him many years to acknowledge and override this force in his decision-making process. He eventually realized that more expensive did not always mean better and a good value was more important to his overall financial health.

If you do not have someone in your life who meets these four criteria, I suggest you contact a pastor in your church or even the accountant at a local church. The people can probably recommend a financial advisor as many churches use a financial advisor for their own finances. Most financial advisors will applaud your efforts and some may even be willing to freely give you some of their time to help you succeed.

Finally, for most people it is extremely helpful to have an accountability partner; but there are exceptions to every rule. You may be the type of person who is much more motivated by a goal written on an index card and taped to your bathroom mirror than by anything someone else may say or do. That's okay. Only you know what works best for you.

One of the greatest lessons you can learn during any self-discovery process is how to identify your own weaknesses and what it takes for *you* to overcome them.

IT'S YOUR TURN!

Congratulations! You should either have just completed or are about to complete your first month's spending plan. So, we have a few extra things to do this week:

1. It's time to evaluate your first month's spending plan and decide if any revisions need to be made for next month.
2. Write your second month's spending plan. (Don't forget to take into consideration any special events happening next month that will require separate funds.)
3. If you have not already done so, ask someone to be your accountability partner.

CHAPTER REVIEW

By the end of this lesson you should have:

✓ Recapped your first month's progress and identified anything positive or negative that needs to be revised in your monthly spending plan.

✓ Written your second month's spending plan.

✓ Identified and asked someone to be your accountability partner.

✓ Set aside your third week's allotment toward your $500 in frozen assets for a total of $150.

WEEK SIX:
SOME FAVORITE RECIPES

In week four, I showed you a relatively painless way to lose the weight of your debt. Just as with food diets, the less drastic your lifestyle changes are, the slower your financial weight comes off. The opposite is also true. When you are willing to make some drastic changes in your lifestyle, you can achieve dramatic financial weight loss in a much shorter amount of time. Many of these changes will take courage and a determination to change your life for the better, much like real weight loss does. I promise, though, that once you see and feel the positive effects of dramatic financial weight loss, you will know how much making these changes was worth it!

The following is a list of ideas on how to reduce your current debts:

1. ***Eliminate your auto loan payment.*** This can be done either by selling the vehicle or turning in a leased vehicle. Even if you had to lose a little bit of money on the resale, it will pay off in all of the interest you'll save from the debts you pay off early!

(Using our example, this single action would eliminate $9,700 of John & Jane's current debt and free up $389 a month toward eliminating their other debts.)

Real-life example: Through a friend, we were able to turn in and replaced a leased vehicle—using *cash* from our income tax return—with a modest, reliable vehicle bought at a local auto auction.

2. **Refinance your mortgage.** If you have a thirty-year mortgage on your home, you could end up paying as much as $250,000 more for your home than if you had a fifteen-year mortgage instead. It is important to compare the interest rate you already have to what might be available right now; but, in general, the monthly difference in your payment will not be more than $100, and you will end up significantly reducing the amount of debt you owe much faster.

    Hint: Even if you don't refinance, you can still pay off your loan in the fifteen-year period by making thirteen payments a year instead of twelve. This can be done relatively painlessly by making half a payment every two weeks or by adding an extra 10% towards the principle in ten of your regularly-scheduled payments throughout the year.

3. **Get a roommate.** If your housing expense is more than 25% of your income, it's too high. Consider getting a roommate to help with the expenses or consider moving to a less-expensive place.

4. **Review your payroll tax withholdings.** If you are receiving a large income-tax-return check at the end of the year, call the payroll department of your company and have your W-2 deductions increased. Having this money every paycheck can help keep you within your monthly calories plan or help to systematically eliminate your debts. You are much less likely to make a major purchase or spend that tax return unwisely if you put this money into your weekly budget instead of receiving it in one lump sum.

5. **Temporarily stop making contributions to your 401(k) or retirement plans.** (Initially, just plan on doing this for a set period of time. For example, one year.) In the long term, you will be much better off

to concentrate on eliminating your debts first, and then planning for retirement.

Note: In some cases, you can borrow money from your own retirement plan to pay off debt. This can be an acceptable option in eliminating your debts because you pay the interest to yourself instead of the credit card companies and because the loan is set up for a finite number of payments (such as twenty-four months) instead of as revolving credit. I do not usually recommend this alternative, however, because of the tendency to use this as a temporary bandage on the problem of overspending. This ultimately leads to even greater financial problems. Also, you may end up paying taxes twice on the same income, if you aren't careful. If you decide to look into this, just know that you must use this option with extreme caution.

6. **Pack your lunches, freeze extra dinner meals, and quit eating out.** This is huge! Nowhere in your budget will you probably be able to find more available cash flow than in the money you spend on eating out and/or fast food. If you must eat out, skip the drinks and just get water. Most restaurants charge almost $2 for a soft drink.

7. **Buy generic groceries and prescriptions.** Most of the generic products are exactly the same as the brand name. This includes health and beauty products, as well. By doing this, we were able to reduce our grocery bill as much as $60 a week without even noticing a difference in the quality of the products.

    Hint: Nowhere can you blow your debt diet faster than in the grocery store. So, every time you shop, make a list of the items you need before you go and stick to it! Check the clearance shelves and the Manager's Special shelves. There are usually great deals on day-old breads and last-day meats, which are fine if frozen before using. Also, don't shop hungry or with small children.

8. **Use generic services.** For example, if you need to color your gray hair for your mental health, then color your own or go to the local beauty school and have it done inexpensively instead of paying $75-$100 in a luxury salon.

9. **Hold a yard sale.**

10. **Shop at yard sales.**

11. ***Shop the Goodwill® store, Salvation Army® store or thrift shop near rich neighborhoods.***

12. ***Be a smart, plan-ahead consumer.*** Most products have a peak season of the year. As much as you can, buy products off-season. For example, if you know that you need new patio furniture, buy it in October or January, not in May through August. This includes services as well. For example, a house painter will give you a much better price for his services during his slower months, such as January, than he will during his busiest time of year.

13. ***Don't pay for unnecessary features.*** Many times, the more-expensive models of appliances have the same motor as the less-expensive model. The more-expensive model just has more "bells and whistles." Before deciding which model to purchase, carefully consider which of the extra features you will actually use. Often the more features an item has, the more opportunities there are that something can break. This can ultimately lead to it costing even more because of expensive repair bills.

14. ***Sell an unnecessary vehicle such as a motorcycle or boat.***

15. ***Reduce your monthly utility bills.*** Contact your local utility companies about ways to make your home more energy efficient and reduce your monthly bills. It could be some things as wearing an extra layer of clothing and turning down the thermostat a few degrees during the winter months or installing a "smart" thermostat that monitors the temperature while you are away from home that could save you hundreds of dollars throughout the year. The utility companies usually have many of these ideas posted on their websites.

    Additionally, don't be afraid to shop around for utility companies. You might find out that you have other companies available for your electricity; internet; trash pick-up, etc. Get quotes from all of them to make sure you are getting the best price available in your area. Sometimes a quick phone call to your local carrier letting them know that you've been offered a lower rate from one of their competitors is all it takes to get your provider to match that lower rate.

16. ***Stop paying club fees.*** Instead of paying membership fees at the local fitness club, most public schools will allow people to use their track before and after school hours. Also, many community centers and parks & rec. departments offer exercise classes and sports facilities for pennies compared to the fitness centers' prices. You are already spending your tax dollars for these services; why not take advantage of them?

17. ***Get a part-time job.*** Even if it only seasonal or temporary, it could dramatically help speed up the process of your financial weight deduction.

    Hint: Make sure that you plan your meals ahead of time; otherwise all the extra money you make from your part-time job will go to pay for fast food because you are too busy or too tired to plan/cook your meals.

18. ***Make your gifts***. Instead of buying gifts for friends and family, decide that for one whole year you are going to give all homemade gifts or recycle perfectly nice things that you already own and give them as gifts to someone who might enjoy them as well.

Hint: Be careful that your homemade gift ideas are cost-effective and that you are not spending as much on the materials as you would have spent if you had just gone out and bought a gift.

19. **Use your entertainment dollars wisely.** If you want to eat out, go out for lunch or dessert and coffee or just appetizers and cocktails instead of a full-course dinner. You will still have an enjoyable time without the large bill to go with it. If you want to see a movie, don't go at seven p.m. the night it premiers when the tickets are $12 each. Go to a matinee showing or to the local dollar movie theater or rent a movie and skip the drinks and popcorn. If you want to buy the latest bestseller, try getting it from your local library first. If you must purchase it, buy it from the local used bookstore or through an online seller.

   Hint: Many local library systems now have online access; and you can put a book from any of the library's branches on hold through your home computer. They will even transport it to your nearest library location and notify you when it is available for you to pick up.

20. **Don't spend loose change**. Put it in a jar instead, and when the jar is full, put the money into your

frozen assets or use it to pay down your debt. It is a small way to save money that you will not even notice.

21. **Be critical of your spending habits.** You need to honestly evaluate what your true needs are versus what you are spending needlessly on luxuries. For example, getting a weekly manicure is not a necessity. A $3 gourmet coffee every morning is not a necessity. Buying and wearing dry-clean-only clothing is not a necessity. (Add just these small items together and we are quickly into hundreds of dollars a month!) In the next lesson we will talk about the occasional treat; but for now, if you are serious about losing your debt, then you need to be willing to forgo some—if not all—of these "little luxuries," even if it is only temporarily.

Real-life example: One couple we worked with committed one year to giving up these little luxuries. They ate modestly and bought several jigsaw puzzles for entertainment, but in *only twelve months* they had saved $18,000 toward the purchase of their first home.

IT'S YOUR TURN!

How committed are you to your goals? Brainstorm at least six actions that you could take to dramatically reduce your own debt and remember to set goals with dates and put them on your calendar.

_____

_____

_____

_____

_____

_____

_____

_____

_____

_____

CHAPTER REVIEW

By the end of this lesson you should have:

✓ Come up with a list of several ideas to speed up your own debt reduction

✓ Made your fourth installment toward your $500 frozen assets for a total of $200.

WEEK SEVEN:
THE OCCASIONAL TREAT

Most dieters can attest to the fact that a diet is much easier to stick with if an occasional treat is built in and planned for. The same will be true for your debt diet. It will be much easier for you to stick with your plan if you have something "just around the corner" to look forward to. Try to have something lined up at least every six to eight weeks. This will give you enough time to build the cost slowly into your spending plan, but still be close enough to get excited about. These don't need to be anything extravagant, but definitely more than just a box of Popsicles on grocery day. Below are some suggested ideas.

1. ***A Day Trip to a Local Tourist Attraction:*** These are usually a good option because you probably know someone or some way to get free or discounted tickets; and there aren't a lot of travel and hotel expenses involved. You'll still spend some money, but it won't be a bank-breaking trip.

2. ***A Trip to a Historical Site:*** Some of my most memorable trips are to places that didn't cost a lot of

money to visit. They were trips to historical sites that usually have very minimal entry fees. These national treasures are really enjoyable; and you might even learn something new!

3. **A Minor-League or High-School Ball Game:** Again, someone you know might be able to get discounted tickets; and even if you can't, the tickets are usually much more reasonably priced than major-league games. Depending on what you have budgeted, you may want to eat before going into the park to keep from paying $4 or more for a hotdog.

4. **Camping Trips:** Borrow a tent from a friend and go camping! Campsites are usually a few dollars a night, and many state and national parks offer beautiful hiking trails. Some even have pools, lakes, horseback riding, and reasonably-priced boat and cabin rentals.

5. **Vacationing College Style:** You've heard about college students who tour Europe with only a few hundred dollars and a bicycle. Well, you don't have to be a college student or in Europe to learn from their money savvy. Some colleges open their

dormitories to vacationers for the summer for as little as $6 a night all over Europe and the United States. A quick look at websites or a phone call should let you know if the college near your favorite vacation spot has any available rooms.

6. **Community Symphony Concerts and Theatrical Performances:** Don't overlook what is going on in your own hometown. Many of the productions happening at your local high schools, churches, and community centers are extremely well done and are either free or charge a nominal entrance fee. This includes the military bands that tour the country. Again, your tax dollars are already paying for many of these events, so why not use them to your advantage and show a little civic pride at the same time?

Occasionally some event arises that you would really like to do, but just didn't have time to budget for. I call this the *unexpected dinner guest* because friends and family are notorious for dropping these things on us at the last minute! In order to say yes to these unexpected opportunities, it is necessary to have a reasonable amount of money (such as

$20-$40) budgeted in your monthly spending plan that is simply allotted as "Entertainment Money".

Hint: We build into our monthly spending plan a few dollars every week of pocket money for my husband and I that we do not have to give an explanation for how it was spent—a soft drink or coffee here or there, a pack of gum or a new pen, etc.—just the little things that we may buy that will not significantly impact our debt reduction.

On a rare occasion, Michael and I would receive an invitation that just not financially an option; and we had to say no. It didn't happen very often, however; and we assured ourselves that it was only a temporary restriction and that our first priority had to be our debt weight loss. These rare invitations served as tests of our commitment to be debt free. Ultimately, they helped solidify our resolve to change our lives for the better!

IT'S YOUR TURN!

What are some fun, inexpensive treats you could build into your plan to help you stay on track? List at least four:

_____

_____
_____
_____
_____
_____
_____
_____
_____
_____
_____

CHAPTER REVIEW

By the end of this lesson you should have:

✓ Listed a couple of fun activities you can build into this month's (and possibly next month's) spending plans as special treats to help you stay on track.

✓ Set aside your fifth allotment toward your $500 of frozen assets for a total of $250. Congratulations! You are halfway there!

WEEK EIGHT:
BEWARE OF TEMPTATIONS

Just as with a food diet, you are going to be faced with temptations every day. Every commercial establishment has its own ways of tempting you to spend your money. They even have their employees attend classes on how to learn suggestive selling techniques and other strategies to part you from your money. Millions of dollars every year are spent on advertisements that are designed with the sole purpose of creating a desire in you to spend your money.

You don't have to hate advertisers and business owners for what they do; you just constantly need to be aware of their intent and on guard for all of these subtle and not-so-subtle attempts to convince you that you *need* to spend your money.

Be especially aware of what advertisers say about debt and credit. Credit is one of the hottest-selling items on the market, and big companies are paying big money to convince you that you need their product. It seems that the credit companies are always coming up with new gimmicks to entice you to get more credit and convince you that you need it. Advertisers will often make statements such as, "Go ahead, you deserve it!" or "You'll earn money (points) by using our credit card." or "You will earn great rewards if you use our credit product."

Often these advertisements sound like a good decision on the surface, but if you really compare the numbers of using their credit product to using cash, cash is always going to be a smarter financial choice. As you become accustomed to dissecting the advertisements and analyze them for any truth they may contain, you will begin to see the fallacies in what they are saying; and the temptation to use these products will be less.

One critical step you must take toward successfully handling these temptations is to identify and know your own weaknesses. Much like food diets, you have to know what your weaknesses are so you can avoid them. If you are on a food diet and your weakness is donuts, then you have to avoid going to the donut shop or down the bakery isle in the grocery store where they stock the donuts. The time for discipline is in the store, not once you've gotten home with the donuts!

If you are tempted to needlessly spend money through catalogs, then throw the catalogs away without opening them or ask to be taken off of their mailing lists. If you know that you can't resist buying shoes, then don't go to the shoe store unless it is absolutely necessary. Here you *must* be honest with yourself and identify these weaknesses early on so they don't cause pitfalls later.

Hint: Your friends, accountability partner, or spouse can probably tell you what your weaknesses are even if you don't know them yourself!

Here is a list of some questions that you can use to help you evaluate temptations as they arise:

1. Is this purchase something I am going to regret buying in two weeks or a month? (aka Buyer's remorse)
2. Can I truly afford this purchase, or is it going to destroy this month's spending plan?
3. Do I really need this, or do I just want it?
4. Is this a purchase that I need to make right now, or can it wait until I can build the expense into my next month's spending plan?
5. What could I do with the money if I didn't make this purchase?
6. Is this item going to end up in my yard sale next year?

7. Can I make a financially healthier choice than buying this item?
8. What would my accountability partner tell me to do?
9. What would I say to someone else in my financial situation who was thinking about making this same purchase?

Hint: This final question is the litmus test for many gray-area questions in life. A decision will always be clearer when you are being asked what someone else in the same situation should do because it is the way to take your emotions out of the choices.

I am not asking you to become a martyr and never allow yourself any flexibility; but I am asking you to be actively disciplined on your own behalf. If you learn to identify the triggers that make you fail, then you can learn how to avoid them.

Hint: One of the easiest steps you can take to force yourself to stay within the spending limits of your monthly spending plan is to leave your ATM, debit, and credit cards at home. *Only take cash with you when you go shopping!* This is the best kind of self-enforced discipline.

IT'S YOUR TURN!

Write the questions listed above on an index card or piece of paper and put it in your purse or wallet, or type the list of questions onto the electronic notepad in your phone and make it your screensaver (at least temporarily) to get you in the habit of asking yourself these questions before making a purchase.

Pay special attention to the advertisements that you see and hear this week, especially for credit. Make a note of any that initially seemed like sound, healthy financial decisions; but, upon closer analysis, are not really very healthy financial choices. List them below and share them with your accountability partner.

_____
_____
_____
_____
_____
_____
_____

Write down at least five situations that you can think of in which you are tempted to spend money. Beside each item write some creative ways you can avoid these temptations.

_____

_____

_____

_____

_____

_____

CHAPTER REVIEW

By the end of this lesson you should have:

- ✓ A deeper awareness of how advertisers and businesses attempt to entice you and what situations tempt you personally.
- ✓ A written list of several creative ways you can guard yourself against these temptations.
- ✓ Set aside your sixth allotment toward your $500 of frozen assets for a total of $300.

WEEK NINE:
KEEP ALL FOOD ON THE TABLE

In week eight, we talked about being tempted to needlessly spend money. There are always going to be times when you don't intentionally make a mistake, but it happens anyway. But then there are going to be times (or have already been times) when you intentionally decide to break the rules—rules that you put in place yourself—in other words, when you *decide* to cheat.

So, if we made the rules ourselves, then why do we intentionally decide to break them?

If we look at some of the reasons why people cheat on a food diet, you will see similar reasons for why people cheat themselves financially.

1. They are depressed or sad and they want to make themselves feel better.
2. They don't want to be embarrassed at a social gathering by not doing what everyone else does.
3. They rationalize the cheat by saying, "Oh, just this once won't hurt."

4. They get depressed by past failures and convince themselves that this is the way they are always going to be, so why try to change?
5. The item is in front of them, and they don't have the willpower to leave it there.

In these examples, you will notice two important qualities that both food and money evoke in people: emotional responses and rationalized thinking.

EMOTIONAL RESPONSES

Have you ever heard of comfort foods? These are the foods that people sometimes eat to warm a sick body or soothe a hurting soul. These foods are being eaten to satisfy other needs in a person instead of satisfying his or her actual physical hunger.

Studies have also shown that the human body actually has a physiological response to spending money. The eyes dilate, the pulse quickens, breathing gets faster, adrenaline production increases—shopping is exciting! For most people shopping is a lot of fun!

To some people, shopping is more than just a necessity. It is their therapy. When shopping itself becomes the problem, then a downward emotional cycle can happen very quickly. In order to combat this use of shopping to meet an emotional need, you must learn to recognize the emotional triggers that make you want to go shopping, and then learn to either avoid the triggers or substitute another relaxation activity that is healthier for your emotions and your wallet.

RATIONALIZED THINKING

The toughest part about food diets and financial diets is that food and money are necessary evils. It is not enough to say that you are never going to eat again or spend money again. Unlike the alcoholic, who can walk away and survive without taking another drink in his life, you will always be faced with having to spend money your whole life. Therefore, you *must* learn to control your spending, and that can only come when you learn to control your thoughts about money.

One way to guard against cheating on a food diet is to keep all food on the table. In other words, no sneaking it when no one is looking. The same holds true for money. Keep all purchases out in the open. Don't hide any purchases from your spouse or accountability partner. This will go a long way in keeping you truthful and honest about what you are spending money on and why.

Your possessions do not define who you are. Being financially healthy will have a much greater impact on your self-worth than any possession you may own.

Probably the climax of your success will come on the day when you completely understand money's role in your life and you wholly believe that a particular purchase is just not worth the headache and heartache it will cause by messing up your financial goals; so you put the item back on the store shelf and walk away. That will be the day when you are completely in control of your spending habits. It will be the day when you know that you are in control of your money instead of your money being in control of you.

Note: Many jokes have been made about "shopaholics," but a true addiction to spending money is no laughing matter; it could ruin your life! If you (or your family) believe that you are a chronic, compulsive shopper, you may want to seriously consider seeking professional help. It should be considered a real addiction, taken seriously, and treated just as you would treat any other addiction.

IT'S YOUR TURN!

You are doing great! This week you should either have just completed or are about to complete your second month's spending plan. So, before we get started on next week's lesson, we have a few exercises to do:

1. It's time to evaluate your second month and decide if any revisions need to be made in the coming month's spending plan.
2. Write your third month's spending plan. (Don't forget to take into consideration any special events happening next month that will require separate funds.)
3. Write down at least three situations that you can think of where you feel the emotional triggers to cheat on your financial diet. Include any ideas you have on how to avoid these situations.
4. List any times when you rationalize your thoughts about spending. Include any statements you can make ahead of time to counter these thoughts.

_____
_____
_____

_____

_____

_____

_____

_____

CHAPTER REVIEW

By the end of this lesson you should have:

✓ Recapped your second month's progress and identified anything positive or negative that needs to be revised in your monthly spending plan.
✓ Written your third month's spending plan.
✓ A better understanding of the emotions and thoughts that tempt you to cheat on your financial diet.
✓ Listed several creative ways you can guard yourself against cheating.
✓ Set aside your seventh allotment toward your $500 of frozen assets for a total of $350.

WEEK TEN:
CONQUERING SET BACKS

One of the toughest challenges to any kind of a diet is sticking with it and toughing it out—no matter what—until you meet your goal. Unfortunately, along the path toward being debt free, you are probably going to meet with some obstacles. (Some of these obstacles, as we discovered in last week's lesson, we may even create ourselves.)

Realistically, you need to expect that setbacks will happen. If you mentally prepare yourself for them ahead of time, then when they do occur, you will not be so defeated emotionally. This attitude will help you to keep the trauma to a minimum and get you back on track much faster. To paraphrase an old saying, *a loss (or in this case a setback) is only a temporary affliction. Quitting is the only thing that makes defeat a permanent condition.*

Some examples of setbacks might be incurring medical bills, the need to repair or replace a vehicle, or the loss of a job. It is quite amazing how any one of these types of incidences can set a financial plan back by months or even years. Yet it doesn't mean that the goal is a total loss.

Time is critical though. Try not to allow yourself to stay off course for too long. The longer you wait to regroup, the harder it will be to feel like you are back on a solid path again. Remember *any* plan is better than no plan at all.

SO, HOW DO YOU CONQUER SETBACKS?

1. Allow yourself (temporarily) to feel and express the full range of your emotions.

Whether we like it or not, finances evoke powerful emotions. Those emotions are natural and very real. It is natural to feel afraid or to feel depressed, to get angry or to cry when something unexpected happens. Those feelings need to be released. Denying or suppressing those emotions will only prolong your recovery process. The faster you can express those feelings and deal with them, the faster you will be able to focus and find a practical solution to getting back on track.

2. When the situation requires it, be forgiving.

Whether it is momentary carelessness or weakness, whether it was ourselves or someone else, let's face it; we all make mistakes. If we add blame, guilt, or shame onto the top of a financial setback, we will clutter our ability to understand the root of the cause and hinder our efforts to work toward a solution. If you need to, apologize. Admitting your own faults and mistakes will help clear the air and better equip you to move on.

3. Be flexible.

In lesson three, I said that your monthly spending plan would be a constant work in progress. It is important to recognize that a setback may require that some adjustments be made to your monthly plan, even if only temporarily.

Real-life example: Michael and I were making visible progress toward paying off our debt when an unexpected home repair become necessary which depleted what we had saved up in our frozen assets. We were able to look at our spending plan and see where we had already rolled the payment of one paid-off medical bill into a student-loan payment. We temporarily stopped making this extra payment onto the student loan and used that money to conquer the setback and replenish our frozen assets. Yes, it momentarily slowed down the progress of our debt payoff, but in a few short months, we were able to add that money back toward our debt reduction.

4. Don't lose sight of your goal.

Much of the time, whether we realize it or not, our drive or energy to accomplish a goal is produced by attitude and momentum. You may have known someone (or done it yourself) who was beginning to achieve some real success on a diet or an exercise plan, and then an injury occurred; they lost their momentum and quit. Remaining focused on your goal will allow you to keep temporary setbacks in the perspective of the whole picture. Keeping your goal in front of you will also help to keep you from dwelling on past mistakes, which can lead to depression.

5. Start over.

There may come a time when you've accomplished your goals of being debt free. You are cruising along and all of a sudden something happens and your financial train gets derailed. Or maybe it happens so gradually that you didn't even realize it, and you find yourself at the bottom of a pile of debt once again. What now? Well, go back to what worked for you before and start the process again. It's okay. It may not be the ideal situation, but it can be dealt with.

WHAT CAN I DO TO GUARD AGAINST SETBACKS?

1. Maintain frozen assets.

The key to your long-term success in guarding against setbacks is going to be your frozen assets. I cannot stress enough how important these funds are ultimately going to be to your lifelong success in overcoming the debt cycle.

2. Don't count on it!

When it comes to your financial plan, optimistic budgeting can be devastating. For example, even if you have received a bonus every August since you've been with the company, it doesn't mean you will get one this year. Don't make these kinds of "probably" funds a part of your budgeting until they become a reality.

Only create your spending plan on the minimum income that you are certain about. Have a plan for what you will do with the extra funds if they materialize, but don't factor them into your monthly and weekly bills or—this is the tough one—into your vacation or holiday funds either.

3. Don't put it off.

Maintaining your home, your vehicles, and your body are good ways to avoid large repair bills later. (Example: Change your car's oil every 3-5,000 miles to keep the engine from wearing out faster.) If you notice a small problem, don't wait until it is a big problem to have it looked at or taken care of.

Real-life example: We noticed a leak in our home-office roof, so we used our frozen assets and had it repaired as quickly as possible in order to avoid extensive wall damage and large repair bills down the road.

Making repairs can be very depressing because they can be a large expense without the feeling of making any progress. But in many cases, procrastinating could end up costing thousands of dollars and set your goals of being debt free back even farther. Don't wait!

4. Evaluate setbacks.

Analyze how and why setbacks happen. Without pointing any fingers, look for either faulty planning in your spending plan or possibly a lack of planning. This will help to keep you from making those same mistakes again.

IT'S YOUR TURN!

Write down at least three creative ways you can personally help yourself conquer a setback.

_____

_____

_____

_____

_____

Write down at least three ideas on how to help yourself avoid a setback.

_____

_____

_____

_____

_____

_____

_____

_____

Write down the things that motivate you to achieve your financial goals. Post this list in your car or on your mirror (somewhere where you will see it every day) to help you stay focused.

_____

_____

_____

_____

_____

_____

_____

_____

_____

_____

_____

_____

_____

_____

CHAPTER REVIEW

By the end of this lesson you should:

✓ Have an understanding of what it will take for you personally to conquer any setbacks you may encounter.
✓ Recognize that a temporary setback is probable, but it does not equate to a permanent failure. You should mentally prepare yourself for those setbacks so you can get back on the right track faster.
✓ Have an idea of what your own weaknesses and pitfalls are so that you can hopefully avoid some of them on the road to your own financial success.
✓ Have set aside your eighth allotment toward your $500 of frozen assets for a total of $400. Keep up the great work! You only have two more weeks to go!

WEEK ELEVEN:

EXERCISE

Almost everyone agrees that exercise plays an integral role in the success of any diet regimen. It helps to speed up your metabolism so you can lose the weight faster; it builds self-confidence; alleviates stress, and gives you a more positive outlook; it strengthens you and supports your efforts to lose weight.

Much like a food diet, your ability to exercise with regard to your finances is going to play an important part in your financial success. We are going to focus on three kinds of exercise: *strength, flexibility, and endurance.*

BUILDING STRENGTH

Build the Strength of Your Financial Knowledge

The more you know about the financial world around you and the better you understand the way economics works and the tools that you have available to you, the better you will be at making smart financial choices. Your decision to work through this book is a great example of how you are gaining financial knowledge, which will help you make even smarter choices. Keep going with this process!

Week twelve will list several financial self-help books. Get them. Read them. Learn from the examples these authors share and take heart the advice they are giving. These experts know what they are talking about, and they have used their methods for proven financial success to help thousands of people just like you.

I heard a professor say once, "If you think education is expensive, try ignorance." Nowhere is this truer than with what you know and don't know about money. Over time, you will gain countless rewards for any time or money you invest in educating yourself about the financial world.

Build the Strength of Your Determination

Strength training requires that you push yourself to the limits of what you think you can achieve and then push yourself beyond that level.

You will build the strength of your determination by setting a smaller goal, pushing yourself to achieve that goal, then setting your sights even higher. (For example, once you have achieved your goal of $500 in frozen assets, then set an even higher goal of $1,000 in frozen assets.)

Step by step, as you continue to achieve each goal, your resolve will strengthen and you will be more determined than ever to see your ultimate financial goals fulfilled—such as the ones we only dreamed about in the introduction!

You can achieve great success at any age, but it won't just happen. You have to make it happen for yourself. And you can only do this with a focused determination to succeed.

BUILDING FLEXIBILITY

In order to exercise your flexibility, you will need to stretch yourself to the limits of your courage and your creativity.

Setting a tough goal takes courage to reach for because there is always the possibility of failure. Yet, you must tell yourself that the achievement of that goal is definitely worth the effort. Setting the tough goal of getting out of debt is definitely worth the effort in order to live completely debt free and move toward fulfilling your deepest-set goals!

Think back on the moments in your life that stand out in your memory the most. Chances are they are the moments when you found the courage to stick your neck out, take a risk, and reach for a goal.

Reaching that goal may mean stretching your brain to its creative limits. The brain is a muscle and, like most of your muscles, needs some time to stretch and warm up to work effectively and at its optimum capability. So, if you can't think of a creative resolution to a financial issue, set the problem aside and come back to it again in a few hours or the next day. Let your mind toss the problem around for a while. Your creative muscles might surprise you on the second or third time you exercise them!

BUILDING ENDURANCE

Endurance training requires the repetition of an action over a long period of time. The more you repeat an exercise, the more fluid and smoother it becomes; the fewer mistakes you make; the easier it is to perform well, and the more confidence you will have in your ability to perform it well. These same principles apply to your ability to execute your monthly financial plan. Each month you will see it becoming easier to live by, with less mistakes and revisions. Your confidence will increase and your excitement will grow as you see yourself gaining control of your finances.

The strength of your endurance will also be built through your ability to recognize, learn, and put into action the successful habits of other people around you.

Real-life example: We know a California man who made millions of dollars off the purchase of one piece of property simply because *he did some research* through the city for upcoming highway plans; *he was patient with his investment,* and *he recognized its true potential.* I now try to incorporate these successful habits into my own financial decisions as well.

Just as an exercise regimen follows a healthy progression toward improved distance or speed, you must work toward your improved, healthier financial picture by setting goals. Most people cannot stay motivated to run five miles every day unless they are training for some kind of race. The same is true for your exercising. Building goals into your financial routine is critical to staying focused and motivated.

Hint: For momentum's sake, you may want to break down large financial goals into smaller, achievable stages, such as monthly or weekly instead of annually.

Another way to stay motivated is to record your progress. Keeping a printed copy of your monthly spending plan is a good way to quickly look back at your progress. Debts that have been complete paid off, salary increases, etc. will be reflected in these statements.

In addition, it is a good idea to occasionally go back to week one's lesson and plug in the current numbers for your assets and obligations. Compare the new version to the worksheet you did at the beginning. These records will act much like a dieter's before and after photos to give you visible data on your progress and can be a powerful motivator to keep you working toward improving those numbers!

NO PAIN, NO GAIN!

Any kind of self-improvement requires periodic examination of the actions being taken and critical analysis of their effectiveness. Sometimes this criticism can come from you, but it may also need to come from someone else. Be cautious about who you ask to provide this, but then be emotionally prepared to openly listen to that person's opinion about how you are handling your money. Criticism—especially of how we handle our finances—is not easy to accept. Try to remember that in any kind of learning process, there is going to be some form of pain involved. This kind of constructive pain, however, will ultimately lead to a more successful approach to your finances and a happier, healthier you!

IT'S YOUR TURN!

Brainstorm about ways that you can exercise to change your current financial situation. Write down anything that comes to mind. Spend *at least* 20 minutes doing the following exercises; this will give your brain time to warm up and get those creative juices flowing!

_____

_____

_____

_____

_____

Answer the questions listed below to jumpstart your creative thinking:

1. Are there any specialized hobbies or skills that you enjoy or are especially good at? If so, list some ways this skill can be marketed to sell as a product or service to others.

   _____

   _____

   _____

   _____

2. Are any of the books on your bookshelves about subjects that are important to you or hobbies that you love? Often a passion for a subject can lend itself to a new financial opportunity.

_____
_____
_____
_____
_____
_____

3. Whom do you know that could help you hone your skills and find a way to market them?

_____
_____
_____
_____
_____
_____

Hint: Don't forget to check your local library for books or Google® or YouTube® to help you do this.

4. What are the qualities in you that other people recognize and admire? How can these qualities be used to boost the metabolism of your debt reduction?

___

5. Look back at the past eleven weeks. Honestly analyze how you have done with meeting your financial goals. List three things that you could do to improve how you are executing your monthly spending plan.

_____
_____
_____
_____
_____
_____
_____
_____
_____
_____
_____
_____
_____
_____
_____
_____

CHAPTER REVIEW

By the end of this lesson you should:

- ✓ Understand how to build the strength of your financial knowledge.
- ✓ Understand how to build the strength of your determination.
- ✓ Have brainstormed several ideas on how to market your skills.
- ✓ Understand how to build the endurance necessary to successfully reach your financial goals.
- ✓ Have set aside your ninth allotment toward your $500 of frozen assets for a total of $450. Keep it up! You are almost there!

WEEK TWELVE:
CONGRATULATIONS! YOU DID IT!

Do you feel different? You should. You have accomplished something that millions of people only dream about. You have successfully taken control of your money.

Do you look different? Your financial snapshot should be starting to take a much healthier shape. Not only have you stopped gaining weight; but you have created a systematic plan and are losing the weight of your debt.

As your shape changes and your new financial habits become part of who you are and how you think, the unhealthy habits of other people around you will become even more obvious. Each time you see the anxiety caused when someone's credit card gets declined or see the agony of a couple fighting over money, you will renew your motivation to never let yourself be in that situation again. As you witness the people around you make poor financial choices and see the disastrous results, you will be more convinced of how necessary it is to your own success that you stay diligent and keep making smart choices. The past eleven weeks have been leading up to this moment. Like a child learning to make his or her own way, you are ready to strike out on your own and find your own paths to success.

This is not a twelve-week fad diet; it is an entire lifestyle makeover. Now it is up to you to keep this plan rolling toward your goals! This is an especially dangerous transition time because it would be easy for you to return to your old spending habits. Remember that the only way to keep yourself from slipping backward into your old habits is to keep intentionally striving forward with a planned strategy.

Often you will see when people are able to lose fifty pounds or more off of their physical weight that their whole lives are changed, not just their physical appearances. They are no longer defeated. They have been empowered, and this confidence overflows into every aspect of their lives. By finding determination to follow this plan for the past twelve weeks, you have learned that you too can accomplish great things in your life.

In the very beginning, I asked you to think about what you could do if you didn't have any debts at all. I asked you to dream. I hope that the confidence and success you have achieved over the last eleven weeks will lead you to achieve even greater things—lead you to the things you have always dreamed of. The goal of realizing your dreams is what will keep motivating you to strive forward, if you remain focused.

ONE FINAL THOUGHT

With all of this talk about money, I don't want you to think that the amount of money you have will define who you are. It won't. Nor do I want you to think that more money will make you happy. It won't do that either. The accumulation of money should not be your ultimate goal.

The definition of success and happiness are individual for each person. Think about the people that you truly admire. What is it about them that you admire? Chances are it is not their houses or their cars that make you feel the way you do; it is more likely some aspects of their characters that you look up to.

I hope that these are the aspects in your life that you will spend your time striving to achieve. When you are able to see the same traits in your own character, then you will find your true happiness and success.

IT'S YOUR TURN!

1. Write down at least three financial goals that you want to accomplish in the *next* twelve weeks. (Example: Another $500 saved toward your frozen asssets!) Remember to write the deadlines on your calendar.
2. Pick at least one book from the following list that you will get and read in the next month.
   - ❖ *The Principle of the Path* by Andy Stanley (Nashville, TN: Thomas Nelson, 2011)
   - ❖ *The Total Money Makeover* by Dave Ramsey (Nashville, TN: Thomas Nelson, 2014)
   - ❖ *Smart Couples Finish Rich* by David Bach (Boston: Crown Publishing Group, 2018
   - ❖ *The 7 Habits of Highly Effective People* by Stephen R. Covey (NY: Free Press, 2003)
3. Do you want to go a step further? Try solely using a cash system for a while. Don't even use a debit card. Get used to always using cash, and it will empower you even more.

4. Write down at least three people that you admire and what characteristics in them you find worthy of your admiration. Ask yourself how well you can see these same traits in your own character or how you can obtain them.

_____
_____
_____
_____
_____
_____
_____
_____
_____
_____
_____
_____
_____
_____
_____
_____
_____

CHAPTER REVIEW

By the end of this lesson you should have:

✓ Identified several characteristics that will lead to your own personal happiness.
✓ Written three new financial goals for the next twelve weeks.
✓ Chosen at least one book from the previous list that you will read next month.
✓ Set aside your tenth and final installment toward your $500 of frozen assets! Congratulations! You did it!

A FINAL REVIEW

In the last twelve weeks you have:

- ✓ Written a list of your assets and liabilities/obligations
- ✓ Determined what being financially healthy means to you personally.
- ✓ Written down both short-term and long-term goals with deadlines.

- ✓ Learned how to apply the reverse goal-planning principle.
- ✓ Categorized your monthly obligations into recurring bills and disposable debts.
- ✓ Prioritized your monthly obligations in order of importance.
- ✓ Successfully written a spending plan for three full months.
- ✓ Identified someone and asked them to be your accountability partner.
- ✓ Created an initial plan as to how you are going to systematically eliminate your debts and put that plan into action.
- ✓ Come up with a list of several ideas to speed up your

own debt reduction.
- ✓ Created a list of fun activities that you can build into your monthly plan as special treats to help you stay on your debt-elimination diet.
- ✓ Learned the necessity of having frozen assets set aside for when the inevitable events of life occur.
- ✓ A deeper awareness of how advertisers and businesses attempt to entice you and what situations tempt you personally.
- ✓ Listed several creative ways you can guard yourself against these personal temptations.
- ✓ A better understanding of the emotions and thoughts that will tempt you to cheat on your financial diet.
- ✓ Listed several creative ways you can guard yourself against cheating on your debt-elimination diet.
- ✓ Created a list of several ideas on how to market your skills.
- ✓ An understanding of what it will take for you personally to conquer any setbacks you may encounter on your road to success.
- ✓ Recognized that a temporary setback does not equate to a permanent failure.

- ✓ Some ideas of what your own weaknesses and pitfalls are so you can avoid some of these things on the road to your own financial success.
- ✓ Created a list of things that motivate you to achieve your financial goals and posted it somewhere where you will see it every day to help you stay focused.
- ✓ Learned how to build the strength of your financial knowledge and your determination.
- ✓ Gained an understanding of how to build the endurance necessary to successfully reach your financial goals.
- ✓ Set aside $500 in frozen assets!

APPENDIX I

SOME FACTS YOU SHOULD KNOW ABOUT DEBT CONSOLIDATION LOANS AND CREDIT COUNSELING AGENCIES

Over the past several decades, consumer credit has become a booming industry. In recent years, two new businesses have emerged within the consumer-credit industry that are gaining popularity both with business owners and the general public: (1) Lenders offering debt consolidation loans and (2) credit counseling agencies. We see them advertised on television and magazines almost constantly. Initially, they sound like smart business decisions; but, in reality, they are apt to do more harm than good. Let's look at each one separately and see why.

DEBT CONSOLIDATION LOANS

This is where a third-party company lends you the money to pay off all or most of your current creditors and roll all of the payments into one monthly payment. Most of the time, these types of loans are secured by the equity in your home and are drawn up as a second (or third) mortgage. This is important to take into consideration for several reasons:

> The loan will put a lien on your home, which could mean the possibility of foreclosure if you were unable to make the payments.

> These types of loans tend to be stretched out over a much longer period than the time it would normally take to pay off a credit card. This means that you must take into consideration the total amount of interest you will be paying over the life of the whole loan, not just what percentage rate the company is offering you.

> If you eventually decided that you needed to file bankruptcy, these types of secured loans are not eligible for consideration during bankruptcy proceedings unless you are willing to relinquish ownership of your mortgaged property.

If you do consolidate your debt without closing your current accounts, it leaves you vulnerable to the temptation to create even more debt. In the long run, this will seriously jeopardize your financial welfare by creating an even larger amount of debt that you will eventually have to pay back.

CREDIT COUNSELING AGENCIES

These agencies are third-party companies that negotiate better interest rates for your current debts and take over your bill-paying process. You send them biweekly or monthly payments, and they distribute these funds to each of your creditors. Again, on the surface this may sound like a smart decision, but there are some important facts you should consider before enlisting the help of this type of company.

No one works for free. These agencies are making money, and you are ultimately the one paying for their services.

As soon as you add a third party to any type of negotiations, things are always going to get more complicated, not simplified. These agencies will initially contact your creditors and negotiate a better rate; but after that, you will be forced to mediate any correspondences that need to happen between the agency and your creditors.

Any time you enlist the help of a credit counseling agency, your credit report is immediately red-flagged. It's possible that lenders see this act as a confirmation of your inability to responsibly handle your own debts.

The credit counseling agency will stay on your permanent credit record for ten years *after your final debt is paid in full.* This means that you will potentially have to live with this mark on your credit record for ten to twenty years!

We live in a society that wants a quick fix for everything, and these types of agencies are preying on your desire to have an instant cure. I hope that by now you realize that the best way for you to handle your debts is to do it yourself. With patience, diligence, and determination, you *can* pay off your debts. It just may take some time.

APPENDIX II

WHAT YOU CAN DO ABOUT HARASSING CREDITORS AND COLLECTION AGENCIES

The business of collecting a debt has been around for centuries. Collection agencies are a part of a credit-driven society, and thousands of people every day have to deal with them. You must understand and remember that a debt collector's <u>only objective</u> is to get you to pay the debt owed to the creditor. Some collectors do not care how they go about getting you to pay, so long as they are successful. They will make you burn with anger or flood the room with tears if that is what it takes for them to get their money.

No one enjoys dealing with creditors or collection agencies; but, in the event that you must deal with them, it is always a good idea to be prepared. Probably your greatest asset in dealing with these agencies is knowledge. Most people know that they owe the debt and therefore assume that they are at the collector's mercy. What most people do not realize is that there are laws in place to protect you, the consumer.

In 1977, the United States Congress passed a law called the Fair Debt Collection Practices Act. This law and its contents are public documents and can be accessed via the internet and possibly at your local library as well. I have highlighted many of the important measures below.

The law very clearly states what a debt collector can and cannot do with regard to how they go about attempting to collect a debt. Your ability to quote these rights, if and when a debt collector calls you will be your greatest defense against the collector's unscrupulous collection practices:

- If you notify the debt collector *in writing* that you wish for them to cease further communication with you, the debt collector may not communicate with you with respect to such debt (except to notify you that further efforts are being terminated or that certain privileges are being revoked) (Section 805-c)
- A debt collector must not call your residence before 8 a.m. or after 9 p.m. your local time (Section 805-a1).
- A debt collector is not to call you at your place of employment (Section 805-a3).

- A debt collector cannot notify you of his or her attempt to collect a debt either by postcard or by any indicators on the outside of an envelope (Section 804-4&-5).
- If the debt collector knows that you are being represented by an attorney, the debt collector cannot contact you personally unless he or she cannot reach the attorney after a reasonable period of time. (Section 805-a2).
- A debt collector may not communicate with *anyone* except you or your attorney or a consumer reporting agency about any debt that you owe (Section 805-b).
- A debt collector cannot harass, oppress, use abusive or obscene language, or threaten physical violence or damage to your reputation in an attempt to collect a debt (Section 806).

These are just some of the highlights that are listed in this law. I encourage you to familiarize yourself with the law so that you will know if and when a debt collection agency oversteps its legal rights.

In addition, if you feel that your rights are being violated, know that you cannot bring a suit against a collector unless you have proof. It is always a good idea to record any conversations you have with these agencies, just remember to notify the person to whom you are speaking that the call is being recorded.

If a debt collector calls, you need to be as brief as possible. You must try not to become emotional. Tell him or her when you will make your next payment and for how much that will be. Remember that you need to take care of your basic needs and have a debt reduction plan in place, be honest and let the collector know what your plan is. (Example: "I will send you $25 on March 15th.") Only you can decide the amount that you can pay them while still taking care of your basic necessities.

You may be asking, "What if the collector says that amount is not good enough?"

This is very likely to happen. You need to remain calm and simply state again that this is the amount you can pay at this time.

Some collectors will threaten to ruin your credit score. Do not be scared by this. If they are calling you, then your credit report has already been flagged, so paying the debt right now will not improve or fix your credit today. The only way to fix your credit is to have regular, consistent payments over time.

It is always a good idea for you to initiate any communication with your creditors. If you are contacting them, they will have less of a need to contact you. Write them a letter via certified mail explaining what you area able to pay and when. Usually—even if you are not making the minimum payments—as long as you are making some amount of a monthly payment, they will stop calling you constantly. Remember, their only goal is to collect your money. So, if you are sending at least a small payment each month, the collectors will spend their time trying to collect from those who aren't making any payments at all.

www.ingramcontent.com/pod-product-compliance
Lightning Source LLC
Chambersburg PA
CBHW070258230526
45470CB00002B/631